Where Do The
Stars
Go
AF569248

ANJAN ROY

BlueRose
Publishers
NewDelhi • London

First Published in January 2022

ISBN: 978-93-93809-44-5

BLUEROSE PUBLISHERS

www.bluerosepublishers.com

info@bluerosepublishers.com

+91 8882 898 898

Cover Design:

Geetika

Typographic Design:

Namrata Saini

Distributed by: BlueRose, Amazon, Flipkart

Chapter 1

My brother Ranjan was what one would call a regular guy.

He may not have been the best human in the world (though I thought he was) but he was definitely a good dada.

Not because he pampered me (in fact I wish he had) but because he lived his life on his terms, at the same time managed to find time for folks whom he hardly knew (for that matter those whom their own folks hardly knew either).

Has it ever occurred to you, how is it that our universe is constantly expanding with millions of stars being born all the time?

Ranjan was one such star that shone pretty much on his own accord and not merely reflecting light like the celestial planets that most of us are.

It's been close to 60 years since Ranjan was born and 30 years since he was reborn a star and continues to shine brighter each day.

I'd love boasting Ranjan's academic achievements which were no mean feat, but I would rather leave it for a later day, because I am excited to share his humane qualities, as he was a good human and a good person first.

Ranjan went away from my life when I was busy cutting classes and chasing girls in pigtails, the year was 1981 if my memory serves me right.

He moved to St Stephen's College to study Physics with the ultimate goal of pursuing Astrophysics in post grad level.

He was a crazy guy who would be out on a freezing Delhi winter's night, a torch/candle in hand and one of his voluminous books depicting diagrammatic representations of various constellations.

Every night Mom would serve dinner and all of us i.e.; especially Dad and me waited impatiently for Ranjan to join us (me irritably of course) as the chapattis were going cold despite lavish ghee slapped on them.

Oh! Ranjan, he drove me mad with his choice of lifestyle, music and books (which I secretly began to read, to gain brownie points over my friends, who were still stuck on James Hadley Chase and Westerns not to miss Archie's and Commandos).

I must admit the Solzynetzyn , Sakharov, Dostoevsky not to miss Tolstoy, Jean Paul Satre and Alberto Moravia were at times uninteresting and depressing, but I read them all the same to gain Dada's approval (which sadly did not come).

I was surprised Ranjan did not express shock when he saw me with his prized possessions. (Maybe he hadn't given up on kid brother altogether).

In fact one of his last BDP ('birth day present', over 3 decades prior to social media type abbreviations) as he referred to them, was a book by Stephen Hawking ' The Brief History of Time, God hadn't I made innumerable attempts to finish reading it. I was overwhelmed to see my son Ranjan Jr reading it few years back. (Seems he was destined to do so, a gift from his namesake ' Jethu').

His choice of music was the ultimate inexplicable, ranging from Bade Gulam Ali khan ,Bismillah Khan, Amjad Ali Khan to Mozart ,Bethovan, Tchaikovsky and for easy listening Deep Purple, Doors ,Pink Flyod ,Traffic, Jethro Tull and CCR ('Creedence Clearwater Revival ' for all you ignoramus).

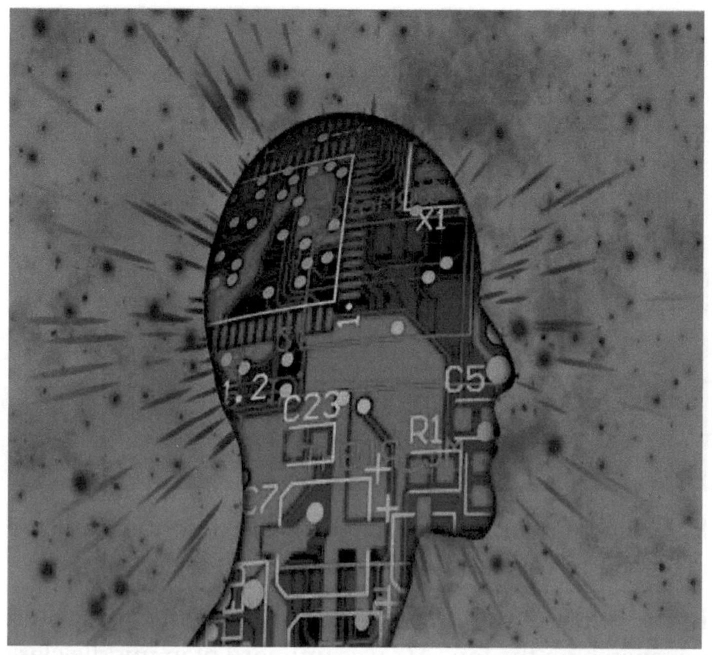

For a regular guy like me , I slowly graduated from ABBA, Boney M to the Beatles (though I secretly still pine for these) and ultimately to his choice of aforementioned Hard Rock. (Even till today my prized possessions of Ranjan's are, his gifts of 'The best of Doors' and 'Traffic' in form of LPs (Long Playing records) which I haven't managed to play since Ranjan became a 'Star', as I am yet to come across a turntable on which I could listen to these beauties after over three decades.

Lifestyle is not an appropriate word to describe Ranjan's life as there was more of life and less of style.

In the midst of blistering Delhi summer, the guy would not switch on the fan (AC was unheard of in middle class houses) and not drink refrigerated water ...Why? Yes, that's what any sane person would ask, and the answer was simple, ' since most Indians don't even have access to clean water, and so it would be inappropriate for me to indulge in such luxuries '. (The guy was a boy of mere 17 yrs, only 2 and half older than me).

He drove me nuts and I dunno about my folks but I was exasperated with ' Dada ' as I seldom referred to him, despite my Mom and Dad's persistent prompting. (It's so nice to hear Maya my daughter referring to Ranjan Jr her brother as Bhaiya or Bhaiyo as she prefers).

Notwithstanding frequent bouts of asthmatic attacks since his early teens, when Ranjan had to be rushed to AFMC (Armed Forces Medical Clinic) near Rastrapati Bhavan each summer, the boy did not give up on pumping iron or for that matter excelled in soccer and badminton too. The guy was very fit and looked real cool effortlessly.

Sadly few years later all the cortisones repeatedly injected led to water retention which made his handsome face puffy.

However that didn't stop his list of admirers (esp. PYTs) from growing. I am now totally convinced that even the ones I managed to befriend secretly, pined for Ranjan.

How I resented the guy then. To his credit he just laughed and brushed aside the matter, when I expressed my concerns to him, saying it was a figment of my imagination. (I was sure it wasn't as one of the girls actually confessed it to me.)

A bout of inexplicable madness hit him while pursuing MSc Physics from IIT-Kanpur , the year was probably 1983. Ranjan 'the great idiot ' decided to chuck IIT in his final year and study Eco from JNU! Yes you got me right, not to prepare for IAS to belatedly oblige my parents, but to help out the backward sections of Indians.

Sounds real corny, right? Yes it did to me too. Not because I ever doubted his intentions for a moment, but the manner he was going about it was sheer madness (or so I thought).

Let me try and elucidate to all you sane folks what this guy was trying.

By foregoing some of the best scholarships in the U.S of A which he bagged for pursuing Astro-Physics his first love , Ranjan realized and rightly so that his studying Economics would have more relevance in understanding the state of affairs of the deprived in India.

Yes, this young man of 22 yrs (I think Catch - 22 seems more appropriate) dumps a career in pure Science research and takes to Economics and not appear for UPSC (Union Public Service Commission) which is what most brilliant young minds do, the ones that want to serve the country i.e;

Who in their right mind would pursue Eco if one had such supposedly honourable intentions of doing something tangible for one's Country.

Yes that's why his friends in IIT-K thought him insane (I suspect my folks were pretty disappointed too, but they didn't bring up the matter on the dining table, because that's where all matters worth bringing up were brought up).

So off went Ranjan Roy to JNU to study Economics and yes you guessed right he did excel in this alien subject too (remember he was a science guy all through , since he became a National Talent Search Scholar after excelling in Class X).

JNU was one heck of a place, 'real maast', I wonder how the guys managed to do any serious studies at all.

The Boy's hostel was more like Co-ed ! Discussions ranged from JP's Movement which kicked Indira Gandhi out of office to the Bhumihaars of eastern UP/Bihar, to whom amongst Vladamir Illich Lenin or Josef Stalin was a greater Hero / Villian of the Russkies.

Mao Tse Dong was more admired than hated by the Left dominated JNUites.

There was this RSS right-wing leaning minority who admiringly held on to their own despite the aggressive posturing of Leftists. (Yes the same guys who had en masse dreams of making it to the US, and had not so secretly applied for American visas).

God! The hypocrisy was laughable.

Though if you questioned any of these 'Jholiwallahs' (that includes both sexes) one would get a long dissertation on how the underground Comrades and the down trodden Blacks are gaining political muscle in the U.S and the fate of Detroit auto workers was worse than that of workers in the Soviet bloc (Polish, Hungarian, Czech to name a few) Russian workers were supposedly the happiest of them all. (Sorry, possibly the Cubans were happier). God! What bull...!

So Dada was in the midst of this terribly exciting socio-political and if I may add cultural pantomime.

Late night or to be precise stretching to early morning, heated/ passionate debates ensued in open air cafes (strategically located in between Boys / Girls Hostels so it was legal /morally acceptable to hang out all night).

Ranjan had this senior roomie Mohanty in JNUs Periyar hostel, a real nerd who was constantly immersed in his voluminous course books had no time for the bindass ladies of Girls Hostel (I doubt they had much time for him either, though I suspect he had a real ' Pataskala ' tucked in somewhere and Ranjan thought the same too and we constantly prodded Mohantyda to let us into his secret but he just smiled his toothy nicotine stained smile, which went well with his thick revolutionary beard).

All most everyone cozied up to Mohantyda to bum his prized Prince Henry tobacco (it had a divine flavour). Would you believe what the intellectual perpetually broke guys did, they bought CLASSIC the cheapest cigarettes available (yes the blue/green denim fabric prints which successfully targeted the students boys/girls alike) emptied the tobacco and stuffed it with Prince Henry and dragged deep into the weed to attain nirvana.

Oh! There was this chic ethnic crowd of mostly girls who were very much part of the Delhi's hip party scene some of whom were regulars at the Embassy parties esp. that of Nigeria.

What stories came out of those Embassy romps can't be put on record, but this bindass crowd were basically into having a good time and these parallel bunch of students were the third category, the first and second being the majority UPSC aspirants / GRE - GMAT types and Ranjan and his ilk were the absolute minority.

There was also a minuscule number of married with kids, well that's another story.

So what does 'Bhai' do when he is through with MA Eco , no he doesn't sit for UPSC as stated earlier, nor does he prepare for GRE / TOEFL which he had anyway maxed couple of years earlier, he joins the Eco Faculty at Hindu College in Delhi University, teaching Final Year guys if I recall correctly. (I wonder why I didn't question him about the name of the college bothering him , given his socialistic leanings, any case I suppose he knew better than me who was languishing in Allahabad University.)

So Ranjan Roy ex- Kendriya Vidyalaya Picket ; Secunderabad, ex - Modern School Barakhamba Rd , ex- St Stephens , ex IIT K and MA Eco JNU settled down to teaching Eco to Hinduites.

As a Stephenian he had his fair share of run-ins with his across the road neighbours the Hinduites bhai log, anyway all in good fun I presume.

Yeah! That still doesn't answer the question, 'Where do the stars go ....? '

Ok I'll come to that in due course I promise I haven't forgotten.

Meanwhile why don't you start thinking where are all your loved ones right at this moment (after all they have to be somewhere shouldn't they ?) whom you have lost from this world.

Now that I have you thinking (I presume I have) it'll help you comprehend my firmly held belief , which of course doesn't have a scientific basis at the moment, however before long hopefully someone would indeed prove me right before I join the Stars too.

Chapter 2

A Supernova star was born today to merge with one young Star born in May 1991.

Dad joined Ranju dada in the vast unknown , to shine brightly in the unfathomable ever expanding Universe .

Dad became overtly outgoing with all young persons since Ranjan's passing away , maybe he was unconsciously trying to make up all the lost moments he couldn't spend with his son owing to professional commitments .

I don't want to turn this chapter onto a morbid obituary as I want them to be remembered as two humans aged 83yrs and 27yrs respectively who lived with passion / grace and died with dignity , and would want to be remembered as such.

During his days in Stephen's Boys Hostel I remember going to meet him once, which luckily happened to be ' The Day ' all of Delhi University in general and Stephenians in particular awaited excitedly ' . This was the evening of The Rock Concert.

Well I wasn't sure what to expect, but seeing Ranjan's friends who I presumed were serious academics totally freaked out in eager anticipation got me expectant too.

The bands started tuning their guitars before the auditorium was filled up and to anybody outside it seemed Jimi Hendricks was majorly into his act . The decibel level was deafening to say the least, not that it mattered to anyone in the audience.

The stage was expectedly lit with psychedelic strobe lights and equally expectedly the galleries were dimly lit for the benefit of the young crowd who were far engrossed by themselves than to actually concentrate about the action on the stage.

The guys and girls were high on grass and the smoke hung up on the ceiling like some low forming cirrus cloud in the sky. The band played Highway Star by the Deep Purple and the crowd got onto their feet and when Stairway to Heaven came on, rhythmic clapping started , slowly but surely a low chant was picking up which if one heard carefully above the din and below the hashish cloud , it was 'Cocaine', no the folks weren't asking for marijuana or any similar weed, they wanted the band onstage to play the Eric Clapton number by the same name.

The band obliged not once or twice but a couple of times more if memory serves me right. I suspect they would have had to play that damn song whole night till some sober guy in the crowd yelled, 'how about some Jim Morrison, Doors / Pink Floyd or something.' And guess which number was yelled for an encore, yes you guessed it 'We don't need no education', had me along with the entire crowd screaming for more.

The Stephen's Faculty got the message alright. Sure enough the Organizers were told that it was well past mid-night and the bands better start packing up and guess what , which was the last number played, yes it actually was Cocaine.

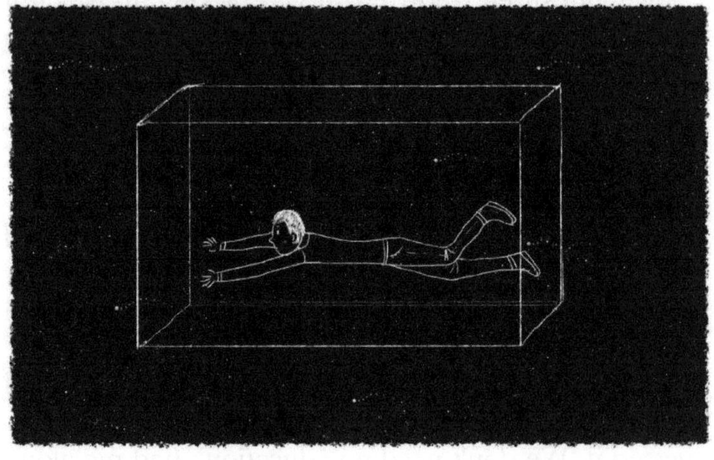

Chapter 3

Academically what Ranjan was up to wasn't anything Enstienian ; however his acute sense of social responsibility wasn't lost on him. We never got to see him during the two month long summer breaks of Delhi University.

Ranjan was away to some non-descript village of Bihar / Haryana during summer along with his equally crazy friends teaching small kids the basics of education , where Government schools didn't exist. I believe these villages had dirt bullock cart tracks which passed off as metalled roads by the bureaucrats of the Ministry of Surface Transport whilst compiling the Annual fictitious statistics for the Govt to present in Parliament.

With the mercury touching over 50 degree centigrade in the Capital, the heat wave conditions in the heartlands of India was oppressively blistering to say the least.

Therefore to voluntarily opt for such 'tandoor' like places was nothing short of insane.

So off went Dada and his idealistic friends to the dusty cow lands of 'Bharat' with steely determination and socialistic dreams of uplifting the poor deprived children of the villages.

These kids who grew up in upper middle class homes , in the capital city of the largest democracy of the World in the comforts of ceiling fans , air-coolers and refrigerators, trooped off happily to spend a fortnight without electricity / water / mosquito nets etcetera.

I was in my final year in school preoccupied with soccer and girls in that order and was least interested in Ranjan's well-meaning socialist leanings.

I suspect a bunch of pretty ladies in tow in the entourage was an added incentive to wander off to God forsaken villages of India.

I bet all of them may not have taken vows of celibacy , not Dada at least I am sure.

Coming to think of it I can think of endless possibilities of naughty fun in the darkness especially with parents safely out of the way in Delhi.

This is in no way to belittle or negate the high ideals and tremendous sacrifices of those college kids , who thought that they could make a difference to the children of Indian villages if not the entire world.

Chapter 4

Sometime during the final year most of the students were busy preparing for GRE / GMAT and TOFEL in full earnest with a view to gain admissions to the best of colleges in the US , there were a few who dreamt of bagging the Rhodes Scholarship to the UK, which one was given to understand was far more prestigious and tougher to get.

Ranjan as expected sailed thru GRE / TOEFL managing admission and scholarship offers from some of the top Institutes to pursue his Masters in Astro-Physics .

Dad and Mom would proudly tell all and sundry of his considerable achievement.

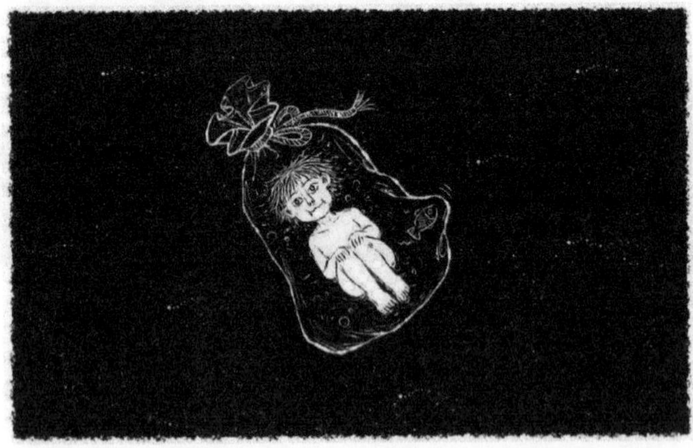

Meanwhile one fine day I heard , he has got admission in IIT; Kanpur (Indian Institute of Technology) and we accepted it as if that was the most obvious thing in the world to do. Nobody wondered as to how come a young man walks into IIT without taking any Coaching classes / Tutorials to crack the JEE (Joint Entrance Examination).

Anyway that's how Ranjan was, topping his class from Pre-Nursery to Class 12, barring Class 11 when he flunked in Physics in his mid-terms and barely clearing Math.

Dad had to write him a long senti letter, reminding Dada how much we all (meaning Dad/Mum) had pinned their hopes on him academically (meaning he was destined to qualify for the Indian Administrative Service) and if his grades dropped any further all would be lost.

Big brother showed me Dad's letter with a remorseful look and for a moment I tried to look equally concerned. Suddenly Bhai burst out laughing so loudly that I was caught totally off guard. That idiot was in splits and he freaked out even more seeing my worried face. “What’s the matter with you he enquired” as if I had plugged in my Boards (which I almost did the following year). “What do you mean, what’s the matter?” I asked.

“You failed in your favourite subject and barely cleared Math, and you are laughing your head off reading Dad's letter”.

I was surprised myself that , I was admonishing Ranjan who all my life was called up by my successive Class teachers to motivate me to study, and here I was expressing concern about his Half-Yearlies.

I was embarrassed to say the least.

“Abbay saley pass ho jaunga na, kyu darr raha hai? Baap ko bol to just relax and take it easy.”

Epilogue

Ranjan kept his word and passed away a few years later in 1991. Admitted in the ICU of Bara Hindu Rao Hospital, New Delhi few weeks earlier, he managed to convince the doctors to voluntarily discharge him as he had to help his students revise their final year syllabus.

Driving his Enfield Bullet 350cc past AIIMS (All India Institute of Medical Science) he experienced mild respiratory distress and decided to park his bike and walk into Emergency Ward.

He explained his medical condition to the Interns on duty and requested oxygen to be given.

The said Interns whom I presume were academically the topmost medical under- graduates of the country failed to comply with the simple request of Ranjan's.

The young medicos panicked and instead of opening the oxygen valve ended up tightening it , rest as they say is history.

Ranjan's brain was starved of oxygen leading to a stroke, leaning over the oxygen trolley, inducing coma from which he never woke up metamorphosing into a Star aged 27yrs.

9 789393 809445

Printed by Libri Plureos GmbH in Hamburg,
Germany